# cocktails

NEW
HOLLAND

# contents

Cocktails – fun and flamboyant drinks, served in fancy glasses and dressed to impress; drinks of unmistakable drama where decadence and elegance combine.

# introduction

We will guide you through the basics and offer you the tips and tricks of the trade, along with recipes for both classics and exciting original concoctions. We have assembled the best set of cocktails imaginable from our extensive and far-reaching catalogue of drinks.

One of the first thoughts that comes to mind when considering cocktails is how did they end up with such a name? Cocktails have a hazy past, perhaps not surprising considering they can be known to pack a punch!

No one is completely sure where the name derives from – perhaps from dressing a mixed drink with a rooster feather to signify its alcoholic potency, or because it was a concoction of leftovers blended together from the tail ends of other drinks dispensed through a stopcock. There are many competing theories on just how this style of drink developed its name.

Today, cocktails encompass a vast set of mixed and shaken drinks topped with juices, dairy products, sugar syrups and often more alcohol! It is likely that the original 'cocktails' were a set of drinks that had a dash of bitters and were shaken or poured over ice, but this has widened over time to include all sorts of beverages, from mulled wines to mixed drinks and non-alcoholic 'mocktails'.

The cocktail has become a wide and varied set of concoctions that is continually added to by both the passionate and professional alike, as many strive to create a signature drink for a new elegant restaurant or to food-match with modern inventive dining.

If you are a cocktail novice, then start with the classics. They are easily found – either check the 'Classics' chapter, or simply flick through the index and look for a name you have heard before. Make sure you have assembled your equipment (we will guide you through this) and slowly but steadily familiarize yourself with the skills of mixology. If you are the adventurous type, keep detailed notes on the quantities used and begin with varying our original recipes with a new twist – but get to know your classics first and be prudent with the variations, as flavours can quickly go off track and become an expensive exercise if too much goes down the drain. Think seasonally as well – fresh fruits and juices are dynamic and full of flavour when picked and juiced at their natural best, which will make a huge difference. For now, assemble what you have that may be useful as bar equipment and check what you may need to add to your equipment if you are planning a full assault on the skills of the cocktail bar. If you do not have the time or resources to put a working cocktail cabinet together, we will show you the bare essentials. If you go down this path, it is a good idea to select a few cocktails, read the recipes and make sure you have the basic equipment necessary before you invest in bottles of spirits and invite the neighbourhood.

# The Basics

Lets start with the four most common methods of
mixing cocktails: shake, stir, build & blend

To perform all of these mix methods you can use either the basic equipment or the extra equipment. If you wish to start out slowly, then work from the essential list and choose your cocktails carefully. If you wish to set up like the pros, then the extra equipment will provide you with a fully equipped bar ready for all occasions and concoctions.

ESSENTIAL EQUIPMENT FOR A BASIC COCKTAIL BAR

| | |
|---|---|
| Bottle opener | Sharp knife |
| Waiter's friend corkscrew | Cutting board |
| Can opener | Mixing glass |
| Cocktail shaker | Measures (jiggers) |
| Hawthorn strainer | Straws |

EXTRA EQUIPMENT FOR A PROFFESIONAL COCKTAIL BAR

| | |
|---|---|
| Electric blender | Ice bucket |
| Swizzle sticks | Ice scoop |
| Scooper spoon | Coasters and paper towels |
| Spoon with muddler | Fresh hand cloths |

# Glassware

Next are the receptacles for your liquid creations. You can serve cocktails in any type of glass, but the better the quality, and the more sparkling the glass, the finer the appearance of your finished cocktail. Don't use scratched, marked or coloured glasses as they will spoil or compete with the appearance of the cocktail. If you are shopping for glassware, choose three or four basic styles that will see you through a range of cocktails, or fill the shelves with sets of the following glassware.

As a quick guide, here is a list of basic glass styles and their traditional uses.
- Highball glasses are for long, cool, refreshing drinks.
- Cocktail glasses are for novelty drinks.
- Champagne saucers are for creamy, after-dinner-style drinks.
- Spirit glasses and tumblers are for classic mixed drinks.
- Shot glasses are for short, strong drinks that are drunk in one mouthful

All cocktail glasses should be kept chilled in a refrigerator or filled with ice while you are preparing the cocktails.

## TYPES OF GLASSES

| | |
|---|---|
| Beer mug | 340 ml (12 fl oz) |
| Brandy balloon | 650 ml (23 fl oz) |
| Champagne flute | 145 ml (5 fl oz), 200 ml (7 fl oz) |
| Champagne saucer | 145 ml (5 fl oz) |
| Cocktail glass | 90 ml (3 fl oz), 145 ml (5 fl oz), 230 ml (8 fl oz) |
| Cordial glass (embassy) | 1 fl oz (30 ml) |
| Cordial glass (Lexington) | generous 1 fl oz (30 ml) |
| Cordial glass (tall Dutch) | 1½ fl oz (45 ml) |
| Fancy cocktail glass | 7 fl oz (200 ml), 10 fl oz (285 ml) |
| Fancy highball glass | 8 fl oz (230 ml), 12 fl oz (340 ml), 16 fl oz (460 ml) |
| Footed highball glass | 10 fl oz (285 ml), 12 fl oz (340 ml) |
| Footed pilsener plass | 10 fl oz (285 ml) |
| Highball glass | 8 fl oz (230 ml), 10 fl oz (285 ml), 12 fl oz (340 ml) |
| Hurricane glass | 8 fl oz (230 ml), 16 fl oz (460 ml), 23 fl oz (650 ml) |
| Irish coffee glass | 8 fl oz (230 ml) |
| Margarita glass | 5 fl oz (145 ml), 12 fl oz (340 ml) |
| Martini glass | 3 fl oz (90 ml), 4 fl oz (115 ml), 1½ fl oz (45 ml) 8 fl oz (230 ml) |
| Old-fashioned spirit glass | 6 fl oz (170 ml), 7 fl oz (200 ml), 10 fl oz (285 ml) |
| Poco grande glass | 14 fl oz (400 ml) |
| Prism rocks glass | 10 fl oz (285 ml) |
| Salud grande glass | 10 fl oz (285 ml) |
| Shot glass | 1½ fl oz (45 ml) |
| Wine glass | 1½ fl oz (45 ml), 7 fl oz (200 ml |

# Basic Recipes

Sugar syrup is needed in a good cocktail bar, as sugar will not dissolve easily in cold cocktails.

Sweet-and-sour mix, is also known as bar mix, and is an important part of many cocktails.

## SWEET-AND-SOUR MIX
## (MAKES 5 CUPS)

1 egg white (optional)
1 cup (7 oz/200 g) sugar
2 cups (8 fl oz/ 250 ml) water
2 cups (8 fl oz/ 250 ml) fresh lemon juice

**1.**  Whisk one egg white until frothy in a medium bowl.
**2.**  Mix in the sugar, then the water and lemon juice. Beat until all the sugar is dissolved.

NOTE: The egg whites are optional, but will make the drinks slightly foamy. Will keep in refrigerator for about a week.

## SUGAR SYRUP
## (MAKES ⅓ CUP)

2 fl oz (60 ml) water
1 cup (7 oz/200 g) sugar

Place water and sugar in a saucepan and bring to a boil. Reduce heat and simmer gently for approximately 5 minutes until the mixture condenses into a clear, sweet syrup. Cool.

NOTE: You can use immediately or store indefinitely in a sealed container in the refrigerator.

# Stocking Your Cocktail Bar

Again, be guided by buying the ingredients that you need for your favourite cocktails if you do not have the space or the resources to purchase the whole list.

## RECOMMENDED LIQUEURS

Advocaat
Amaretto
Baileys Irish Cream
Banana Liqueur
Benedictine
Curaçao blue
Chartreuse, green and yellow
Cherry advocaat
Cherry brandy
Coconut liqueur
Cointreau
Crème de cacao
Crème de café
Crème de cassis
Crème de menthe
Drambuie
Frangelico
Galliano
Grand Marnier
Grenadine cordial (non-alcoholic)
Kahlúa
Kirsch
Mango liqueur
Melon liqueur
Orange liqueur
Peach liqueur
Pimm's No. 1
Sambuca black
Sambuca clear
Strawberry liqueur
Tia Maria
Triple sec
Vandermint

## RECOMMENDED SPIRITS

Brandy
Campari
Gin
Malibu
Ouzo
Pernod
Rum, dark and light
Southern Comfort
Tequila
Vodka
Whisky, for example, Scotch whisky, Irish whiskey, rye whiskey, Tennessee whiskey, Bourbon
Recommended Vermouth
Vermouth bianco
Vermouth dry
Vermouth rosso

# Juices, garnishes & other ingredients

Almonds, slivered
Apple
Apricot jelly
Banana
Blueberries
Cantaloupe
Carbonated water
Celery
Celery salt
Chocolate flakes
Cinnamon
Cocktail onions, red
Coconut cream
Cream, fresh, single and whipped
Cucumber
Eggs
Fruit, canned
Fruit nectar, canned
Fruit pulp, canned
Jelly babies
Lemon juice, pure

Lemons
Limes
Maraschino cherries, red
Milk
Mint leaves
Nutmeg
Olives
Onions
Orange and mango juice
Oranges
Pepper
Pineapple, canned crushed
Pineapple, fresh
Salt
Strawberries
Sugar and sugar cubes
Sugar syrup
Tabasco
Tomatoes
Vanilla ice cream
Worcestershire sauce

# All the Tricks of the Trade

Read through and practice all of the tips and techniques offered and you will develop a failsafe cocktail technique ready for any occasion, no matter how intimate or elaborate.

# Mixing Methods

SHAKE:

To mix by shaking in a cocktail shaker by hand. Fill the glass part of the shaker three-quarters full with ice, then pour the ingredients on top. Pour the contents of the glass into the metal part of the shaker and shake vigorously for 10–15 seconds. Remove the glass section and, using a Hawthorn strainer, strain contents into the cocktail glass. Shaking ingredients that do not mix easily with spirits is easy and practical, for example, juices, egg whites, cream and sugar syrups.

STIR:

To mix the ingredients by stirring them with ice in a mixing glass and then straining them into a chilled cocktail glass. Short circular twirls are most preferred (the glass part of a shaker will do well for this). Spirits, liqueurs and vermouths that blend easily together are mixed by this method.

BUILD:

To mix the ingredients in the glass in which the cocktail is to be served, floating one on top of the other. Highball, long fruit juice and carbonated mixed cocktails are typically built using this technique. Where possible, a swizzle stick should be put into the drink to mix the ingredients after being presented. Long straws are excellent substitutes when swizzle sticks are unavailable.

BLEND:

To mix the ingredients using an electric blender or mixer. Add the fruit first (using small pieces of fruit gives a smoother texture), then pour in the alcohol. Ice should always be added last. This order ensures that the fruit is blended freely with the alcoholic ingredients and allows the ice to gradually mix in, chilling the drink. Ideally, the blender should be on for at least 20 seconds.

Always check that the blender is clean before you start. Angostura bitters is ammonia-based, so it's suitable for cleaning. Fill with hot water, rinse and then wipe clean.

# Techniques

SHAKE AND POUR:
After shaking the cocktail, pour the contents straight into the glass. When pouring into highball glasses and some old-fashioned glasses, the ice cubes are included. This eliminates straining.

SHAKE AND STRAIN:
Use a Hawthorn strainer to prevent the ice from going into the glass.

FLOAT INGREDIENTS:
Hold the spoon right way up and rest it with the lip slightly above the level of the last layer. Fill spoon gently and the contents will flow smoothly from all around the rim. Use the back of the spoon only if you are experienced.

MUDDLE:
Muddling is the process of crushing or bruising fruit or mint garnishes in a glass with the muddler end of the bar spoon or with a pestle, often with some sugar and a small amount of liqueur. Other ingredients of the cocktail are added after muddling is complete. The muddling process extracts the maximum flavour from the fruit or mint. The drink can be strained after muddling if desired.

FROSTING (SUGAR AND SALT RIMS):
This technique is used to coat the rim of the glass with either salt or sugar. First, rub lemon, lime or orange slices all the way around the glass rim. Next, holding the glass upside down by the stem, rest it on a plate containing salt or sugar and turn slightly so that it sticks to the glass. Pressing the glass too deeply into the salt or sugar often results in chunks sticking to the glass. A lemon or lime slice is used for salt and an orange slice is used for sugar.

To achieve colour affects, put a small amount of grenadine or coloured liqueur in a plate and coat the rim of the glass, then gently place in the sugar. The sugar absorbs the grenadine, which turns it pink. To frost mint leaves for garnish, dip them in water or egg white, then dip both sides in caster (superfine) sugar.

## GARNISHING:

Simplicity is the most important fact to keep in mind when garnishing cocktails. Do not overdo the garnish – make it striking, but if you can't get near the cocktail to drink it, then you have failed. Most renowned cocktails are served simply with a slice of lemon, a twist of orange, or a single red cherry. Tall, refreshing highballs tend to have more garnish as the glass is larger. Plastic animals, umbrellas, fans and a whole variety of novelty goods are available for decorative purposes, and they add a lot of fun to the drink – just remember to be restrained.

Long cocktails should usually be served with a swizzle stick for additional mixing. It's customary to serve straws both with highly garnished cocktails and with cocktails made for women to avoid lipstick rubbing off on the glass.

## HANDLING ICE:

Ice is a vital ingredient of most cocktails and must be clean and fresh at all times. Small, squared cubes and flat chips of ice are better for chilling and mixing cocktails. Wet ice, ice scraps and broken ice should only be used in blenders.

To crush ice, fold the required amount of ice into a clean linen cloth and smash it against a solid surface. Although slightly uncivilized, this is an effective method.

Alternatively, a blender may be used to crush ice. Half-fill the blender with ice and then pour in water until it reaches the level of the ice. Blend for about 30 seconds, strain out the water and you will have perfectly crushed ice. Portable ice crushers can also be purchased from kitchen supply stores.

Always use a scoop to collect the ice from an ice tray or bucket. Shoveling a glass into an ice tray to gather ice can cause the glass to break and should be avoided.

It is important that the ice tray or bucket has been wiped clean before you put any ice into it, to ensure that the ice is always clean and untainted.

## HANDLING FRUIT JUICES:

If you are planning to set up a bar for more than one night, never leave juices,

BACARDI:
A light-bodied rum.

BAILEYS IRISH CREAM:
The best-selling liqueur in the world. It is a blend of Irish whiskey, dairy cream and other flavourings.

BANANA LIQUEUR:
A banana-flavoured liqueur. Serve straight, with ice, soda, or as part of a favourite cocktail.

BOURBON:
A type of whisky with a smooth, easy flavour.

BRANDY:
A smooth and mild spirit, mainly produced from the juice of grapes. It is considered a very smooth and palatable drink and ideal for mixing.

BUTTERSCOTCH SCHNAPPS:
A butterscotch-flavoured liqueur.

CALVADOS:
Fine apple brandy made in Normandy.

CAMPARI:
A bitter Italian aperitif. Suitable both as a long or short drink, or as a key ingredient in many fashionable cocktails.

CASSIS:
A rich purple liqueur that delivers the robust flavour and aroma of blackberries.

CHAMBORD:
A raspberry-based liqueur.

CHARTREUSE:
A liqueur available in yellow or green. Still made by monks of the Carthusian order.

CHERI-SUISSE:
A chocolate- and cherry-flavoured liqueur from Switzerland.

CHERRY ADVOCAAT:
A morello cherry-flavoured, advocaat-based liqueur.

CHERRY BRANDY:
Made from concentrated morello cherry juice with a small quantity of bitter almonds and vanilla added. Enjoyable as a neat drink and a versatile mixer.

CHERRY HEERING:
A dark-red cherry-flavoured liqueur made in Denmark.

COCONUT LIQUEUR:
A smooth liqueur with the exotic flavour of coconut, heightened with light-bodied white rum.

COINTREAU:
A liqueur with the aromatic orange flavour of natural citrus fruits. A great mixer and delightful over ice.

CRÈME DE BANANA:
Creamy yellow liqueur very similar to banana liqueur.

CRÈME DE CACAO DARK:
A rich chocolate liqueur. Smooth and classy. Serve on its own, or mix for all kinds of delectable treats.

CRÈME DE CACAO WHITE:
This liqueur delivers a powerful and full-bodied chocolate flavour. An excellent mixer when a chocolate flavour without colour is desired.

CRÈME DE CAFÉ:
A sweet brown liqueur made from extracts of coffee.

CRÈME DE CASSIS:
A blood-red, sweet, blackcurrant-flavoured liqueur.

CRÈME DE GRAND MARNIER:
A very smooth-tasting premium blend of Grand Marnier and French cream. The orange/cognac flavour blends beautifully with the cream.

CRÈME DE MENTHE GREEN:
A liqueur with a clear peppermint flavour, reminiscent of a fresh and crisp winter's day in the mountains. An excellent mixer.

CRÈME DE MENTHE WHITE:
The same flavour as crème de menthe green, for when colour is not required.

CURAÇAO BLUE:
Slightly bitter liqueur based on natural citrus fruits. Same as triple sec but brilliant blue colour is added to make cocktails more exciting.

CURAÇAO ORANGE:
Same as curaçao blue, but has a strong orange colour and flavour.

CURAÇAO RED:
Same as curaçao blue, but has a strong red colour.

CURAÇAO TRIPLE SEC:
Also known as white curaçao. As for blue curaçao, but without colour. Can be served with or without ice as a neat drink, and is used in more mixed cocktails than most other liqueurs.

CYNAR:
An Italian bitter aperitif liqueur made from 13 herbs and plants the most significant of which is artichoke.

DRAMBUIE:
A Scotch whisky liqueur, which means, 'the drink that satisfies'. Made from a secret recipe dating back to 1745.

DUBONNET:
A wine-based aperitif from France flavoured with spices and quinine.

**FERNET BRANCA:**
A bitter, aromatic Italian spirit made from over 40 herbs and spices, with a base of grape alcohol. Often served as a digestif.

**FRANGELICO:**
A wild-hazelnut liqueur imported from Italy. Contains infusions of berries and flowers to enrich the flavour.

**GALLIANO:**
A classic golden liqueur that blends with a vast array of mixed drinks. Varieties include anise, liquorice and vanilla.

**GLAYVA:**
A whisky-based honey- and herb-flavoured liqueur from Scotland, similar to Drambuie.

**GRAND MARNIER:**
An orange-flavoured liqueur, a blend of fine Cognac and extract of oranges. The recipe is more than 150 years old.

**GRAPPA:**
An Italian brandy made from distilling grape skins, known as a digestif.

**GRENADINE CORDIAL:**
A traditional thick red cordial with berry-style grenadine-flavour. It is a non-alcoholic syrup.

**IRISH WHISKEY:**
The distinctive national whiskey of Ireland, Irish whiskey is distilled three times, not twice. Made from malted barley, unmalted barley, and other grains such as rye and corn.

**GIN:**
A grain-based spirit; its aroma comes from juniper berries and other subtle herbs. The perfect mixer for both short and long drinks.

JÄGERMEISTER:
A bitter German aperitif flavoured by a complex blend of 56 herbs, fruits and spices.

KAHLÚA:
A smooth, dark Mexican liqueur made from real coffee and fine clear spirits.

KIRSCH:
A fruit brandy distilled from morello cherries. Delicious straight and also excellent in a variety of food recipes.

KÜMMEL:
A liqueur flavoured with caraway and cumin seeds, popular in Russia and Germany.

MALIBU:
A clear coconut liqueur based on white rum. It blends well with virtually every mixer available to create tropical-style drinks.

MANDARIN NAPOLEON:
A Belgian orange liqueur made from cognac flavoured with oils from fresh Sicilian tangerines.

MANGO LIQUEUR:
A mango-flavoured liqueur.

MELON LIQUEUR:
A soft green liqueur with a melon flavour. Serve on the rocks, or use to create summertime cocktails.

MINT LIQUEUR:
A term for any liqueur with mint flavouring, for example, crème de menthe, peppermint schnapps, etc.

OPAL NERA:
See sambuca black.

ORANGE BITTERS:
Bitters made from unripe orange rinds infused in alcohol (see also Angostura bitters).

ORANGE LIQUEUR:
An orange-flavoured liqueur.

ORGEAT:
A sweet almond-flavoured syrup made also with rose water and orange-flower water.

OUZO:
The traditional aperitif of Greece. The distinctive flavour is derived mainly from the seed of the anise plant.

PARFAIT AMOUR:
A light-bodied purple French liqueur made from lemons, oranges, brandy and herbs.

PASSIONFRUIT LIQUEUR:
A passionfruit-flavoured liqueur.

PEACH LIQUEUR:
The delicious flavour of fresh and dried peaches.

PEACHTREE SCHNAPPS:
A clear spirit, with the taste of ripe peaches. Drink chilled, on the rocks or mix with any soft drink or juice.

PEAR BRANDY:
A digestif made from pears, sometimes sold with a pear in the bottle.

PERNOD:
An anise-flavoured French spirit, commonly drunk as an aperitif.

PIMM'S NO. 1:
A gin-based liqueur, flavoured by a secret combination of herbs and spices.

PINEAPPLE LIQUEUR:
A necessity for summertime cocktails.

RUM:
A spirit distilled from fermented sugar. Can be dark or light. Light-bodied rums are popular for cocktails requiring subtle aroma and delicate flavour.

RYE WHISKEY:
Distilled from rye, corn and malted barley. A light, mild and delicate whiskey, ideal for drinking straight or in mixed cocktails.

SABRA:
An Israeli liqueur with a distinct flavour that comes from oranges, with a hint of chocolate.

SAMBUCA BLACK:
As for clear sambuca but flavoured with extracts of black elderberry.

SAMBUCA CLEAR:
An Italian liqueur made from elderberries with a touch of anise.

SCOTCH WHISKY:
The distinctive national spirit of Scotland. Made from malted barley and other grains.

SOUTHERN COMFORT:
A sweet and full-bodied peach-flavoured liqueur based on Bourbon whiskey. Its recipe is a secret.

STRAWBERRY LIQUEUR:
A fluorescent red liqueur with an unmistakable strawberry bouquet.

STREGA:
From Italian origins, Strega is made from sugar, orange peel, spices and strong spirits.

TENNESSEE WHISKEY:
A type of whiskey distinct from Bourbon, made from the 'old sour mash' process.

TEQUILA:
A spirit distilled from the sap of the agave or century plant. A perfect mixer, or drink straight with salt and lemon.

TIA MARIA:
A rum-based liqueur whose flavour derives from Jamaican coffee. It is not too sweet with a subtle taste of coffee.

TRIPLE SEC:
See curaçao triple sec.

VANDERMINT:
A rich chocolate- and mint-based liqueur.

VERMOUTH BIANCO:
A light, fruity and refreshing vermouth. Mixes well with club soda, lemonade and fruit juices.

VERMOUTH DRY:
A crisp, light and dry vermouth, used as a base for many cocktails.

VERMOUTH ROSSO:
This vermouth has a bitter-sweet herbal flavour, and is often drunk as an aperitif.

VERMOUTH:
Vermouth is a herb-infused wine, made in France and Italy. Three styles are the most prevalent: bianco, rosso and dry.

VODKA:
The second highest-selling spirit in the world, generally made from grain or potatoes.

WEST COAST COOLER:
A white-wine-based alcoholic drink with fruit flavours.

WHISKY:
See Bourbon, Irish whiskey, rye whiskey, Scotch whisky and Tennessee whiskey.

# aperitifs

# Allies Cocktail

SERVES 1

**INGREDIENTS**
1 fl oz (30 ml) gin
1 fl oz (30 ml) dry vermouth
1 tsp (5 ml) lemon kümmel

**GLASS**
3 fl oz (90 ml) cocktail glass

**1.** Combine all ingredients in a mixing glass with ice and stir well. Strain into glass.

# Ante

SERVES 1

**INGREDIENTS**
1 fl oz (30 ml) Dubonnet
   Rouge
1 fl oz (30 ml) Calvados

½ fl oz (15 ml) Cointreau

**GLASS**
3 fl oz (90 ml) cocktail glass

**1.** Combine all ingredients in a mixing glass with ice and stir well. Strain into glass.

# Argincourt

SERVES 1

INGREDIENTS
1 fl oz (30 ml) sweet
    vermouth
1 fl oz (30 ml) dry vermouth
½ fl oz (15 ml) amaretto

1 tsp (5 ml) lemon juice

GLASS
3 fl oz (90 ml) cocktail glass

1. Shake all ingredients with ice and strain into cocktail glass.

# Astoria

SERVES 1

INGREDIENTS
1½ fl oz (45 ml) gin
1 fl oz (30 ml )dry vermouth
dash of orange bitters
1 olive

GLASS
6 fl oz (170 ml) old-
    fashioned glass

1. Combine all ingredients except olive in a mixing glass with ice and stir well. Strain into glass, then drop the olive into the glass.

# Bresnan

SERVES 1

**INGREDIENTS**
1½ fl oz (45 ml) sweet
  vermouth
1 fl oz (30 ml) dry vermouth
½ fl oz (15 ml) lemon juice
1 tsp (5 ml) crème de cassis

**GLASS**
3 fl oz (90 ml) cocktail glass

1. Shake all ingredients with ice and strain into cocktail glass.

# Campari & Soda

SERVES 1

**INGREDIENTS**
2 fl oz (60 ml) Campari
2 fl oz (60 ml) soda water
1 slice of orange

**GLASS**
6 fl oz (170 ml) old-
  fashioned glass

1. Build over ice and stir well. Garnish with slice of orange.

# Cardicas

SERVES 1

**INGREDIENTS**
1 fl oz (30 ml) light rum
½ fl oz (15 ml) Cointreau
½ fl oz (15 ml) port

**GLASS**
3 fl oz (90 ml) cocktail glass

**1.** Combine all ingredients in a mixing glass with ice and stir well. Strain into glass.


# Claridge's

SERVES 1

**INGREDIENTS**
1 fl oz (30 ml) dry vermouth
1 fl oz (30 ml) gin
2 tsp (10 ml) apricot brandy
2 tsp (10 ml) Cointreau

**GLASS**
3 fl oz (90 ml) Champagne saucer

**1.** Combine all ingredients in a mixing glass with ice and stir well. Strain into glass.

# Cynar Cocktail

SERVES 1

### INGREDIENTS
1 fl oz (30 ml) Cynar

1 fl oz (30 ml) sweet
  vermouth

½ slice of orange

### GLASS
3 fl oz (90 ml) cocktail glass

**1.** Mix the liquid ingredients with 2–3 ice cubes in the glass. Garnish with orange slice on side of glass.


# Dry Negroni

SERVES 1

### INGREDIENTS
1 fl oz (30 ml) Campari

1 fl oz (30 ml) gin

1 fl oz (30 ml) dry vermouth

lemon twist

### GLASS
6 fl oz (170 ml) old-
  fashioned spirit glass

**1.** Combine all liquid ingredients in a glass almost filled with ice and stir well. Garnish with the lemon twist dropped into glass.

# Dunlop

INGREDIENTS
1½ fl oz (45 ml) light rum
1 fl oz (30 ml) dry sherry
dash of Angostura bitters
1 piece lemon peel

GLASS
3 fl oz (90 ml) cocktail glass

**1.** Combine all liquid ingredients in a mixing glass with ice and stir well. Strain into glass.
**2.** Squeeze lemon peel over the drink then add the peel to the glass.

# Gilia

SERVES 1

INGREDIENTS
1½ fl oz (45 ml) Aperol
1 fl oz (30 ml) Scotch whisky

GLASS
3 fl oz (90 ml) cocktail glass

**1.** Combine all ingredients in a mixing glass with ice and stir well. Strain into glass and serve with a stirrer.

# Imperial

SERVES 1

### INGREDIENTS
1 fl oz (30 ml) gin
1 fl oz (30 ml) dry vermouth
dash of Angostura bitters
dash of maraschino liqueur
1 olive

### GLASS
3 fl oz (90 ml) cocktail glass

**1.** Shake all liquid ingredients with ice and strain into cocktail glass. Spear the olive with a cocktail stick and add to the glass.

# Little Princess

SERVES 1

### INGREDIENTS
1 fl oz (30 ml) light rum
1 fl oz (30 ml) sweet vermouth

3 maraschino cherries

### GLASS
generous 5 fl oz (150 ml) tumbler

**1.** Combine all liquid ingredients in a mixing glass with ice and stir well. Strain into glass.
**2.** Spear 3 cherries with a toothpick and lay across glass.

# Parisian

SERVES 1

INGREDIENTS
1 fl oz (30 ml) gin
1 fl oz (30 ml) dry vermouth
2 tsp (10 ml) crème de cassis
lemon twist

GLASS
3 fl oz (90 ml) cocktail glass

**1.** Combine all liquid ingredients with cracked ice in a cocktail shaker and shake well. Strain into a chilled glass and garnish with lemon twist.

# Red Gin

SERVES 1

INGREDIENTS
1½ fl oz (45 ml) gin
2 tsp (10 ml) cherry brandy
1 slice of orange

GLASS
3 fl oz (90 ml) cocktail glass

**1.** Shake all liquid ingredients with ice and strain into cocktail glass. Garnish with slice of orange speared with a cocktail stick.

# Robson

SERVES 1

**INGREDIENTS**
1 fl oz (30 ml) dark rum
½ fl oz (15 ml) grenadine
½ fl oz (15 ml) orange juice
2 tsp (10 ml) lemon juice

**GLASS**
3 fl oz (90 ml) cocktail glass

1. Shake all ingredients with ice and strain into cocktail glass.

# Shaft

SERVES 1

**INGREDIENTS**
1 fl oz (30 ml) Aperol
1 fl oz (30 ml) gin
dry sparkling wine for
    topping up
½ slice of orange

**GLASS**
10 fl oz (285 ml) highball
glass

1. Mix the Aperol and gin with ice cubes in a highball glass. Top up with the sparkling wine. Garnish with the orange slice on rim of glass and serve with a straw and stirrer.

# South Express

INGREDIENTS
*1 fl oz (30 ml) kirsch*
*1 fl oz (30 ml) dry vermouth*
*1 fl oz (30 ml) sweet*
  *vermouth*

*lemon zest*

GLASS
*5 fl oz (145 ml) cocktail*
  *glass*

1. Combine all liquid ingredients in a mixing glass with ice and stir well. Strain into glass. Garnish with lemon zest.

# Velvet & Silk

SERVES 1

INGREDIENTS
*1 fl oz (30 ml) Cynar*
*1 fl oz (30 ml) gin*
*slice of lemon*

GLASS
*3 fl oz (90 ml) cocktail glass*

1. Shake all liquid ingredients with ice and strain into cocktail glass. Garnish with lemon slice dropped into glass.

# crème-based drinks

# Alexander

SERVES 1

**INGREDIENTS**
1 fl oz (30 ml) gin
1 fl oz (30 ml) white crème
de cacao

1 fl oz (30 ml) heavy
(double) cream

ground nutmeg

**GLASS**
3 fl oz (90 ml) cocktail glass

**1.** Shake all liquid ingredients with ice and strain into cocktail glass. Sprinkle grated nutmeg on top of drink.

# Almond Joy

SERVES 1

**INGREDIENTS**
½ fl oz (15 ml) amaretto
½ fl oz (15 ml) white crème
de cacao

2 fl oz (60 ml) heavy
(double) cream

1 cherry

**GLASS**
5 fl oz (145 ml) cocktail
glass

**1.** Blend all liquid ingredients with ice and strain into cocktail glass. Garnish with cherry on side of glass.

# Banshee

INGREDIENTS
½ fl oz (15 ml) banana
liqueur

½ fl oz (15 ml) white crème
de cacao

2 fl oz (60 ml) heavy
(double) cream

GLASS
5 fl oz (145 ml) cocktail
glass

**1.** Blend all ingredients with ice and strain into cocktail glass.

# Bright Eyes

SERVES 1

INGREDIENTS
1 fl oz (30 ml) white crème
de cacao

1 fl oz (30 ml) strawberry
liqueur

1 fl oz (30 ml) vodka
1 fl oz (30 ml) heavy
(double) cream

1 fl oz (30 ml) banana
liqueur

6 ripe strawberries
chocolate flakes

GLASS
8 fl oz (230 ml) martini
glass

**1.** Blend all liquid ingredients with 5 of the strawberries and ice, then pour into the glass. Garnish with the remaining strawberry on side of glass and sprinkle chocolate flakes on top.

# Calcutta Flip

SERVES 1

INGREDIENTS

1½ fl oz (45 ml) dark rum

1½ fl oz (45 ml) light (single) cream

¾ fl oz (22 ml) sugar syrup (see introduction)

2 tsp (10 ml) orange-flavoured liqueur

1 egg yolk

ground nutmeg

GLASS

5 fl oz (145 ml) footed cocktail glass

1. Shake all ingredients except nutmeg with ice and strain into glass. Sprinkle nutmeg on top.

# Cantaloupe Dream

SERVES 1

INGREDIENTS

1 fl oz (30 ml) maraschino liqueur

1 fl oz (30 ml) Galliano

1 fl oz (30 ml) orange juice

1 fl oz (30 ml) heavy (double) cream

3 scoops fresh rock melon, plus 1 rock melon ball

sprig of fresh mint

GLASS

10 fl oz (285 ml) fancy highball glass

1. Blend all liquid ingredients and the 3 scoops of rock melon with ice and strain into glass. Garnish with rock melon ball on side of glass with mint.

# Climax

INGREDIENTS
½ fl oz (15 ml) amaretto
½ fl oz (15 ml) white crème de cacao
½ fl oz (15 ml) Cointreau
½ fl oz (15 ml) banana liqueur
½ fl oz (15 ml) vodka

2 fl oz (30 ml) double (heavy) cream

GLASS
5 fl oz (145 ml) cocktail glass

1. Blend all ingredients with ice and strain into cocktail glass.

# Godson

INGREDIENTS
1 fl oz (30 ml) Galliano
1 fl oz (30 ml) amaretto
1 fl oz (30 ml) heavy (double) cream

ground cinnamon

GLASS
7 fl oz (200 ml) old-fashioned glass

1. Build over ice cubes in glass and stir. Sprinkle with cinnamon dust.

# Gumbo Fizz

SERVES 1

### INGREDIENTS
2 fl oz (60 ml) gin

1 fl oz (30 ml) lemon juice

1 fl oz (30 ml) heavy
(double) cream

1 tsp (5 ml) superfine
(caster) sugar

1 egg white

1 tsp (5 ml) Cointreau

3 fl oz (90 ml) soda water

### GLASS
10 fl oz (285 ml) highball
glass

1.   Shake all ingredients except soda water with ice
and strain into highball glass almost filled with ice
cubes. Add the soda water and stir well. Serve with a
stirrer and straw.

# Love in the Afternoon

SERVES 1

### INGREDIENTS
1 fl oz (30 ml) dark rum

1 fl oz (30 ml) orange juice

1 fl oz (30 ml) coconut
cream

½ fl oz (15 ml) heavy
(double) cream

½ fl oz (15 ml) sugar syrup
(see introduction)

6 ripe strawberries

chocolate flakes

### GLASS
5 fl oz (145 ml) Champagne
saucer

1.   Blend all liquid ingredients with 5 of the strawberries
and ice, then pour into the glass. Garnish with the
remaining strawberry and sprinkle chocolate flakes on top.

# Matinee

SERVES 1

### INGREDIENTS
2 fl oz (60 ml) gin

1 fl oz (30 ml) sambuca
clear

1 egg white

4 dashes of lime juice

1 fl oz (30 ml) heavy
(double) cream

ground nutmeg

### GLASS
145 ml (5 fl oz) martini
glass

**1.** Shake all ingredients except nutmeg with ice
and strain into martini glass. Sprinkle nutmeg on top.

# Multiple Orgasm

SERVES 1

### INGREDIENTS
1 fl oz (30 ml) Baileys

1 fl oz (30 ml) Cointreau

1 fl oz (30 ml) heavy
(double) cream

1 red cherry

ground cinnamon

### GLASS
7 fl oz (200 ml) fancy
cocktail glass

**1.** Build over ice cubes in glass and stir. Garnish
with the cherry and cinnamon.

# Pink Poodle

SERVES 1

**INGREDIENTS**

1 fl oz (30 ml) Campari

1 fl oz (30 ml) dry gin

1½ fl oz (30 ml) double (heavy) cream

4 strawberries

**GLASS**

145 ml (5 fl oz) Champagne saucer

1. Blend all ingredients with ice and pour into glass.

# Pink Squirrel

SERVES 1

**INGREDIENTS**

½ fl oz (15 ml) crème de almond

½ fl oz (15 ml) white crème de cacao

60 ml (2 fl oz) double (heavy) cream

**GLASS**

145 ml (5 fl oz) cocktail glass

1. Blend all ingredients with ice and strain into cocktail glass.

# Silk Stockings

INGREDIENTS
1 fl oz (30 ml) tequila
1 fl oz (30 ml) white crème
    de menthe
dash of grenadine
1 fl oz (30 ml) double
    (heavy) cream

1 red cherry
ground cinnamon

GLASS
5 fl oz (145 ml) Champagne
    saucer

**1.** Blend all liquid ingredients with ice and strain into Champagne saucer. Garnish with red cherry and sprinkle cinnamon dust on top.

# Sombrero

INGREDIENTS
1½ fl oz (45 ml) coffee
    liqueur
30 ml double (heavy) cream

GLASS
17½ fl oz (650 ml) brandy
    balloon

**1.** Shake all ingredients with ice and strain into a chilled brandy balloon.

# Strawberry Tremor

SERVES 1

### INGREDIENTS

1 fl oz (30 ml) strawberry
liqueur

½ fl oz (15 ml) white crème
de cacao

2 fl oz (60 ml) double
(heavy) cream

4 strawberries

### GLASS

5 fl oz (145 ml) Champagne
saucer

1. Blend liquid ingredients and 3 strawberries
with ice and pour into Champagne saucer. Garnish
with remaining strawberry on side of glass.

# Sweet Lady Jane

SERVES 1

### INGREDIENTS

½ fl oz (15 ml) white
curaçao

1 fl oz (30 ml) strawberry
liqueur

1 fl oz (30 ml) double
(heavy) cream

½ fl oz (15 ml) orange juice

½ fl oz (15 ml) coconut
cream

1 strawberry

chocolate flakes

### GLASS

5 fl oz (145 ml) Champagne
saucer

1. Shake all liquid ingredients with ice and strain
into Champagne saucer. Garnish with strawberry on
side of glass and sprinkle chocolate flakes on top.

# White Heart

SERVES 1

**INGREDIENTS**

½ fl oz (15 ml) sambuca
   clear

½ fl oz (15 ml) white crème
   de cacao

2 fl oz (60 ml) double
   (heavy) cream

**GLASS**

5 fl oz (145 ml) cocktail
   glass

**1.** Blend all ingredients with ice and pour into
cocktail glass. Serve with straw and stirrer.

# White Russian

SERVES 1

**INGREDIENTS**

2 fl oz (60 ml) vodka

1 fl oz (30 ml) white crème
   de cacao

1 fl oz (30 ml) double
   (heavy) cream

**GLASS**

5 fl oz (145 ml) cocktail
   glass

**1.** Shake all ingredients with ice and strain into
cocktail glass.

# frozen drinks

# Banana Daiquiri

SERVES 1

**INGREDIENTS**
1½ fl oz (45 ml) light rum
½ fl oz (15 ml) Cointreau
1½ fl oz (45 ml) lime juice
1 tsp (5 ml) sugar
1 medium banana, sliced
lemon twist

**GLASS**
5 fl oz (145 ml) Champagne
flute

**1.** Blend all ingredients except the lemon with
½ cup crushed ice until smooth, then pour into a
Champagne flute. Garnish with lemon twist.

# Blushin' Russian

SERVES 1

**INGREDIENTS**
1 fl oz (30 ml) coffee liqueur
1 fl oz (30 ml) vodka
1 scoop vanilla ice cream
4 large strawberries

**GLASS**
5 fl oz (145 ml) Champagne
flute

**1.** Blend all ingredients except 1 strawberry with
½ cup crushed ice until smooth. Pour into a
Champagne flute. Serve with a straw and garnish
with remaining strawberry.

# Devil's Tail

INGREDIENTS
1½ fl oz (45 ml) light rum
1 fl oz (30 ml) vodka
1½ tsp (7.5 ml) grenadine
1½ tsp (7.5 ml) apricot
  brandy

wedge of lime

GLASS
5 fl oz (145 ml) Champagne
  flute

**1.** Blend all liquid ingredients with ½ cup crushed ice until smooth. Pour into Champagne flute. Serve with a straw and garnish with lime wedge.

# Frozen Blue Margarita

SERVES 1

INGREDIENTS
wedge of lime
salt
4 fl oz (120 ml/½ cup)
  tequila

1 fl oz (30 ml) Cointreau
2 fl oz (60 ml) lime juice
2 fl oz (60 ml) blue curaçao

1 tsp (5 ml) caster
  (superfine) sugar

GLASS
12 fl oz (1½ cups/340 ml)
  margarita glass

**1.** Rub the edge of the margarita glass with the lime wedge and frost with salt. Mix all remaining ingredients in a blender with ice and blend until slushy. Pour into the prepared margarita glass.

# Frozen Cherry Margarita

SERVES 1

INGREDIENTS
wedge of lime
salt
6 maraschino cherries
1½ tbsp (45 ml) tequila
1 fl oz (30 ml) lime juice

1 fl oz (30 ml) maraschino
 liqueur

GLASS
1½ cups (12 fl oz /340 ml)
 margarita glass

**1.** Rub margarita glass rim with lime wedge and frost with salt. In a blender, combine maraschino cherries, tequila, lime juice and maraschino liqueur. Blend until smooth. With the motor running, add ice cubes a few at a time until the mixture becomes thick and slushy. Pour into prepared glass and serve.

# Frozen Daiquiri

SERVES 1

INGREDIENTS
1½ fl oz (45 ml) light rum
½ fl oz (15 ml Cointreau
1½ fl oz (45 ml) lime juice
1 tsp (5 ml) sugar
1 cherry

GLASS
5 fl oz (145 ml) cocktail
 glass

**1.** Blend all ingredients except the cherry with ½ cup crushed ice until smooth, then pour into cocktail glass. Garnish with cherry and serve.

# Frozen Italian Margarita

SERVES 1

INGREDIENTS

2 slices of lime or lemon
salt
6 fl oz (¾ cup/180 ml)
   frozen lemonade
   concentrate

3 fl oz (90 ml) tequila
2 fl oz (60 ml) amaretto
1 fl oz (30 ml) Cointreau

GLASS

12 fl oz (1½ cups/340 ml)
   margarita glass

**1.** Rub the margarita glass rim with 1 lime or lemon slice and frost with salt. Put all liquid ingredients and 1 cup ice in a blender and blend until slushy. Pour into prepared glass, garnish with remaining lime or lemon slice and serve.

# Frozen Kiwi Margarita

SERVES 1

INGREDIENTS

2 wedges of lime
salt
4 fl oz (120 ml) silver
   tequila
4 fl oz (120 ml) triple sec
8 fl oz (250 ml) lemon juice
4 fl oz (120 ml) lime juice

½ cup (3½ oz/90 g) caster
   (superfine) sugar
2 kiwi fruit, peeled

GLASS

12 fl oz (1½ cups/340 ml)
   margarita glass

**1.** Rub margarita glass rim with 1 wedge of lime and frost with salt. Put liquid ingredients, sugar and kiwi fruit into a blender, then add ice. Blend until slushy, pour into margarita glass and garnish with remaining lime wedge.

# Frozen Lavender Margaritas

SERVES 8-10

### INGREDIENTS

8 fl oz (250 ml) tequila

4 fl oz (120 ml) blue curaçao

8 fl oz (250 ml) coconut milk

3 fl oz (90 ml) lime juice

450 g (1 lb) frozen raspberries

450 g (1 lb) frozen blueberries

20 ml (1 tbsp) granulated (white) sugar

1 tsp (5 ml) fresh lavender

wedge of lime

lavender sprigs, rinsed

### GLASS

1½ cups (12 fl oz/340 ml) margarita glass

1. In a blender, combine the first 4 ingredients. Gradually add the raspberries and blueberries. Top up with ice. Blend until smooth and slushy. Put sugar and lavender in a saucer. Mash to release the lavender flavour. Frost glass rims with lime wedge, then lavender sugar. Pour margaritas into glasses. Garnish with lavender sprigs.

# Frozen Mango Margarita

SERVES 1

### INGREDIENTS

wedge of lime

sugar

1½ fl oz (45 ml) silver tequila

1 fl oz (30 ml) triple sec

1½ fl oz (45 ml) lemon juice, freshly squeezed

2 fl oz (60 ml) sweet-and-sour mix (see introduction)

¾ cup mango, partially frozen

1 mango slice

### GLASS

1½ cups (12 fl oz/340 ml) margarita glass

1. Rub rim of glass with lime wedge and frost with sugar. Mix all liquid ingredients with frozen mango and cracked ice in a blender and blend until slushy. Pour into prepared margarita glass. Garnish with mango slice.

# Frozen Matador

INGREDIENTS
slice of lime
salt
1½ fl oz (45 ml) tequila
2 fl oz (60 ml) pineapple
    juice
4 tsp (20 ml) lime juice

1 pineapple spear

GLASS
6 fl oz (170 ml) old-
    fashioned glass

**1.**  Rub rim of glass with lime and frost with salt.
Blend liquid ingredients with 1 cup of crushed ice
until smooth. Pour into old-fashioned glass. Serve
with a straw and garnish with pineapple spear.

# Frozen Papaya Margarita

SERVES 1

INGREDIENTS
slice of lime
salt
1 papaya, chopped
4 fl oz (125 ml) gold tequila
2½ fl oz (75 ml) Cointreau
2 fl oz (60 ml) lime juice

GLASS
1½ cups (12 fl oz/340 ml)
    margarita glass

**1.**  Rub rim of glass with lime and frost with salt.
Purée the papaya until smooth. Place in a small container
and refrigerate for 1 hour.
**2.**  In a blender, add the purée, tequila, Cointreau, lime juice and 1 cup crushed ice.
Blend on high until thick and slushy. Pour into the prepared glass.

# Frozen Strawberry Margaritas

SERVES 4

INGREDIENTS
1 lime or lemon, cut into
   slices

salt
6 fl oz (180 ml) tequila
2 fl oz (60 ml) Cointreau
2 fl oz (60 ml) frozen
   limeade concentrate

1 cup frozen strawberries

GLASS
1½ cups (12 fl oz/340 ml)
   margarita glass

**1.** Rub margarita glass rims with lime or lemon slices and frost with salt. Combine liquid ingredients, strawberries and 8 cups ice in a blender and process until slushy. Pour into prepared glasses, garnish with remaining lime or lemon slices and serve.

# Frozen Watermelon Margaritas

SERVES 4

INGREDIENTS
2¼ lb (1 kg) seedless
   watermelon, cut into
   25 mm (1 in) chunks

1 lime, cut into wedges
salt
6 fl oz (180 ml) tequila

4 fl oz (120 ml) Cointreau
2½ fl oz (75 ml) fresh lime
   juice

GLASS
1½ cups (12 fl oz/340 ml)
   margarita glass

**1.** Freeze the melon chunks in a plastic bag until solid. Rub margarita glass rims with lime wedges and frost with salt.
**2.** Blend the tequila, Cointreau, lime juice and watermelon until fairly smooth. Divide the cocktail mixture among the prepared glasses. Squeeze a lime wedge into each cocktail, drop the wedge into the glass, and serve immediately.

# Frozen Margaritas with Lime

SERVES 6

INGREDIENTS

1 lime, cut into slices

sugar

13 fl oz (380 ml) sweet-and-sour mix (see introduction)

4 fl oz (120 ml) tequila

2½ fl oz (75 ml) papaya nectar

2½ fl oz (75 ml) guava nectar

2 fl oz (60 ml) coconut cream

GLASS

1½ cups (12 fl oz/340 ml) margarita glass

**1.** Rub 6 margarita glass rims with lime slices and frost with sugar. Combine remaining ingredients in a blender with 8 ice cubes and process until well blended. Pour into the glasses and garnish each glass with slices of lime.

# Gulfstream

SERVES 2

INGREDIENTS

slice of orange

sugar

1 fl oz (30 ml) blue curaçao

3 fl oz (90 ml) Champagne

½ fl oz (15 ml) light rum

½ fl oz (15 ml)brandy

6 fl oz (180 ml) lemonade

1 fl oz (30 ml) lime juice

1 strawberry, halved

GLASS

7 fl oz (200 ml) footed tulip

**1.** Rub rim of glass with orange and frost with sugar. Blend liquid ingredients with 1 cup of crushed ice until smooth. Pour into glasses, serve with a straw and garnish with the strawberry.

# hot drinks

# Baileys Irish Coffee

SERVES 1

*INGREDIENTS*
*1 fl oz (30 ml) Baileys*
*1 tsp (5 ml) brown sugar*
*hot coffee*
*whipped cream*
*chocolate flakes*

*GLASS*
*7½ fl oz (230 ml) Irish*
*coffee glass*

**1.** Pour Baileys into glass and stir in brown sugar. Fill to within ½ in (15mm) of top with hot coffee. Cover surface to brim with whipped cream, then top with chocolate flakes.

OTHER LIQUEUR COFFEES: French – brandy, English – gin, Russian – vodka, American – Bourbon, Parisienne – Grand Marnier, Mexican – tequila, Monk's – Benedictine, Scottish – Scotch, Canadian – rye

# Bedroom Farce

SERVES 1

*INGREDIENTS*
*1 fl oz (30 ml) dark rum*
*½ fl oz 15 ml Bourbon*
*2 tsp (10 ml) Galliano*
*4 fl oz (120 ml) hot*
  *chocolate*

*2 fl oz (60 ml) double*
  *(heavy) cream*

*½ tsp (2.5 ml) grated*
  *(shredded) dark*
  *(bittersweet) chocolate*

*GLASS*
*7½ fl oz (230 ml) Irish*
*coffee glass*

**1.** Pour first three ingredients into an Irish coffee glass, then add hot chocolate. Carefully spoon cream on top, and sprinkle with the grated chocolate.

# Black Gold

SERVES 1

*INGREDIENTS*
*4 fl oz (120 ml) black coffee*
*½ fl oz (15 ml) Cointreau*
*½ fl oz (15 ml) amaretto*
*½ fl oz (15 ml) Baileys*
*½ fl oz (15 ml) Frangelico*
*whipped cream*

*chocolate flakes*
*ground cinnamon*

*GLASS*
*7½ fl oz (230 ml) Irish*
*coffee glass*

**1.** Pour first five ingredients into an Irish coffee glass, and stir well. Carefully spoon cream on top, then sprinkle with chocolate flakes and ground cinnamon.

# Black Stripe

SERVES 1

*INGREDIENTS*
*2 fl oz (60 ml) dark rum*
*4 tsp (20 ml) molasses*
*1 tsp (5 ml) honey*
*lemon twist*

*GLASS*
*7½ fl oz (230 ml) Irish*
*coffee glass*

**1.** Pour liquid ingredients and ¼ cup (50 ml) boiling water into an Irish coffee glass and stir well. Garnish with the lemon twist.

# Calypso Coffee

INGREDIENTS
*slice of orange*
*sugar*
*1½ fl oz (45 ml) dark rum*
*hot coffee*
*whipped cream*

GLASS
*7½ fl oz (230 ml) Irish*
*coffee glass*

**1.** Rub rim of glass with orange and frost with sugar. Pour rum into glass and fill to within ½ in (15 ml ) of top with the hot coffee. Cover surface to brim with whipped cream.

# Chocolate Vice

SERVES 1

INGREDIENTS
*1½ fl oz (45 ml) dark rum*
*½ fl oz (15 ml) Bourbon*
*½ fl oz (15 ml) dark crème*
  *de cacao*

*4 fl oz (120 ml) hot*
  *chocolate*

*2 fl oz (60 ml) double*
  *(heavy) cream*

*chocolate flakes*

GLASS
*7½ fl oz (230 ml) Irish*
  *coffee glass*

**1.** Pour first four ingredients into mug, then carefully spoon cream on top. Sprinkle with chocolate flakes.

# Coffee Royal

SERVES 1

**INGREDIENTS**
4 fl oz (120 ml) hot coffee
1 tsp (5 ml) granulated
  (white) sugar

2 fl oz (60 ml) brandy
2 fl oz (60 ml) double
  (heavy) cream

**GLASS**
7½ fl oz (230 ml) Irish
  coffee glass

**1.** Pour coffee in glass and add sugar, stir to
dissolve. Add the brandy and stir well. Pour the
cream carefully on top so that it floats.

# Gin Toddy

SERVES 1

**INGREDIENTS**
1 sugar cube
2 fl oz (60 ml) gin
slice of lemon
ground nutmeg

**GLASS**
7½ fl oz (230 ml) hot wine
  mug

**1.** Place the sugar cube in the glass, pour over
½ cup (120 ml ) hot water and stir well, then add gin.
Float the lemon slice on top and sprinkle over
nutmeg.

# Hot Brandy Alexander

SERVES 1

INGREDIENTS
1 fl oz (30 ml) brandy
1 fl oz (30 ml) dark crème de cacao

4 fl oz (120 ml) hot (but not boiling) milk

whipped cream
chocolate flakes

GLASS
7½ fl oz (230 ml) Irish coffee glass

1.  Pour all ingredients except cream and chocolate into heated mug. Top with whipped cream and sprinkle with chocolate flakes.

# Hot Buttered Rum

SERVES 1

INGREDIENTS
1 tsp (5 ml) brown sugar
4 tsp (20 ml) butter
2 fl oz (60 ml) dark rum
ground nutmeg

GLASS
7½ fl oz (230 ml) hot coffee mug

1.  Place sugar in mug, pour over ½ cup (120 ml) hot water and stir well, then add butter and rum. Sprinkle nutmeg on top.

# Hot Piper

SERVES 1

*INGREDIENTS*
*2 fl oz (60 ml) tequila*
*2 tsp (10 ml ) lemon juice*
*½ fl oz (15 ml) dark crème*
*de cacao*

*4 fl oz (120 ml) hot coffee*

*GLASS*
*7½ fl oz (230 ml) Irish*
*coffee glass*

**1.** Pour all ingredients into Irish coffee glass and stir well.

# Hot Whisky Toddy

SERVES 1

*INGREDIENTS*
*1 sugar cube*
*2 fl oz (60 ml) Scotch whisky*
*slice of lemon*

*GLASS*
*7½ fl oz (230 ml) hot*
*whisky glass*

**1.** Put sugar into glass, pour in ⅔ cup (150 ml ) boiling water, then add whisky and stir. Decorate with a lemon slice.

# Indian Summer

SERVES 1

INGREDIENTS
ground cinnamon
2 fl oz (60 ml) Calvados
¾ cup (6 fl oz/175 ml) hot
   apple cider

1 cinnamon stick

GLASS
7½ fl oz (230 ml) hot coffee
   mug

**1.** Dip rim of glass in ground cinnamon. Pour Calvados and cider into mug, then add cinnamon stick.

# Irish Coffee

SERVES 1

INGREDIENTS
slice of orange
sugar
1½ fl oz (45 ml) Irish
   whiskey

hot coffee

whipped cream

GLASS
7½ fl oz (230 ml) Irish
   coffee glass

**1.** Rub rim of glass with orange and frost with sugar. Pour Irish whiskey into glass and fill to within ½ in (15 mm) of top with the hot coffee. Cover surface to brim with whipped cream.

# Jamaican Coffee

SERVES 1

**INGREDIENTS**
*slice of orange*
*sugar*
*1½ fl oz (45 ml) Tia Maria*
*hot coffee*
*whipped cream*

**GLASS**
*7½ fl oz (230 ml) hot coffee*
*mug*

**1.** Rub rim of glass with orange and frost with sugar. Pour Tia Maria into glass and fill to within ½ in (15 mm) of top with the hot coffee. Cover surface to brim with whipped cream.

# Mulled Claret

SERVES 1

**INGREDIENTS**
*1 sugar cube*
*5 fl oz (145 ml) claret*
*1½ tsp (7.5 ml) lemon juice*
*2 dashes of orange bitters*
*ground cinnamon*

**GLASS**
*7½ fl oz (230 ml) hot coffee*
*mug*

**1.** Stir the sugar into ¼ cup (50 ml ) boiling water until dissolved. Stir in the remaining ingredients and mull with a red-hot spoon before serving.

# long drinks

# Astronaut

*INGREDIENTS*
*2 fl oz (60 ml) dark rum*
*2 fl oz (60 ml) vodka*
*½ fl oz (15 ml) lemon juice*
*1 tsp (5 ml) passionfruit*
    *pulp*

*GLASS*
*9 fl oz (285 ml) highball*
*glass*

**1.** Shake all ingredients except passionfruit pulp with ice, and strain into glass. Drop passionfruit pulp into glass.

# Bahama Mama

*INGREDIENTS*
*½ fl oz (15 ml) light rum*
*½ fl oz (15 ml) Malibu*
*½ fl oz (15 ml) banana*
    *liqueur*
*½ fl oz (15 ml) grenadine*
*2 fl oz (60 ml) orange juice*

*2 fl oz (60 ml) pineapple*
*juice*

*wedge of pineapple*

*GLASS*
*9 fl oz (285 ml) highball*
*glass*

**1.** Blend liquid ingredients with ice and pour into glass. Garnish with pineapple wedge and serve with a straw.

# Blue Bayou

SERVES 1

INGREDIENTS
1 fl oz (30 ml) gin
½ fl oz (15 ml) Galliano
½ fl oz (15 ml) dry
  vermouth
½ fl oz (15 ml) blue curaçao
lemonade

slice of lemon
mint leaves

GLASS
9 fl oz (285 ml) highball
  glass

1.   Shake first 4 ingredients over ice and pour into glass. Top up with lemonade. Garnish with the lemon slice and mint leaves. Serve with a straw.

# Blue French

SERVES 1

INGREDIENTS
1 fl oz (30 ml) Pernod
½ fl oz (15 ml) blue curaçao
½ fl oz (15 ml) lemon juice
bitter lemon soda
slice of lemon

GLASS
9 fl oz (285 ml) highball
  glass

1.   Build over ice in glass. Top up with bitter lemon soda and stir well. Garnish with the lemon slice. Serve with a stirrer.

# Bombay Punch

SERVES 1

INGREDIENTS
1 fl oz (30 ml) Cognac
½ fl oz (15 ml) dry sherry
½ fl oz (15 ml) Cointreau
½ fl oz (15 ml) maraschino
  liqueur
½ fl oz (15 ml) lemon juice

sparkling wine
1 red cherry

GLASS
9 fl oz (285 ml) highball
  glass

**1.** Blend the first 5 ingredients with ice and pour into the glass. Top up with sparkling wine and garnish with the red cherry. Serve with a straw.

# Brandy Ice

SERVES 1

INGREDIENTS
1 fl oz (30 ml) brandy
½ fl oz (15 ml) vanilla
  extract
2 scoops vanilla ice cream
½ fl oz (15 ml) lemon juice
bitter lemon soda

slice of orange
1 strawberry

GLASS
9 fl oz (285 ml) highball
  glass

**1.** Blend the first 4 ingredients with ice and pour into the glass. Top up with bitter lemon soda and garnish with the orange slice and strawberry. Serve with a straw and stirrer.

# Canadian Daisy

INGREDIENTS
1 fl oz (30 ml) Canadian
  Club whisky

½ fl oz (15 ml) brandy
½ fl oz (15 ml) lemon juice
1 tsp (5 ml) grenadine

soda water
1 cherry

GLASS
9 fl oz (285 ml) footed
  highball glass

**1.** Shake the first 4 ingredients with ice and pour into glass. Top up with soda water and garnish with the cherry. Serve with a straw and stirrer.

# Chi Chi

SERVES 1

INGREDIENTS
1½ fl oz (45 ml) vodka
½ fl oz (15 ml) coconut
  cream

1 fl oz (30 ml) Malibu
½ fl oz (15 ml) lime syrup
½ fl oz (15 ml) lemon syrup

2 fl oz (60 ml) pineapple
  juice

dash of thickened cream
wedge of pineapple

GLASS
9 fl oz (285 ml) highball
  glass

**1.** Blend liquid ingredients with ice until smooth then pour into glass. Garnish with pineapple wedge. Serve with a straw and stirrer.

# Chiquita

SERVES 1

### INGREDIENTS
1½ fl oz (45 ml) vodka
½ fl oz (15 ml) banana
   liqueur
½ fl oz (15 ml) lime juice
½ banana, sliced

pinch of sugar
bitter lemon soda

### GLASS
9 fl oz (285 ml) highball
glass

**1.** Blend the first 5 ingredients with ice and pour
into glass. Top up with bitter lemon soda. Serve
with a straw.

# Dizzy Blonde

SERVES 1

### INGREDIENTS
2 fl oz (60 ml) advocaat
1 fl oz (30 ml) Pernod
lemonade
slice of orange

### GLASS
9 fl oz (285 ml) highball
glass

**1.** Shake the first 2 ingredients with ice and pour
into the glass. Top up with lemonade and garnish with
orange slice. Serve with a straw and stirrer.

# Frangelico Luau

SERVES 1

INGREDIENTS
1½ fl oz (45 ml) Frangelico
7 fl oz (200 ml) pineapple
     juice
dash of grenadine

slice of pineapple

GLASS
9 fl oz (285 ml) highball
     glass

1. Blend the first 3 ingredients with ice and pour into the glass. Garnish with pineapple slice.

# Freddy Fud Pucker

SERVES 1

INGREDIENTS
1 fl oz (30 ml) tequila
4 fl oz (120 ml) orange juice
½ fl oz (15 ml) Galliano
slice of orange
1 cherry

GLASS
9 fl oz (285 ml) highball
     glass

1. Build over ice in glass and float the Galliano on top. Garnish with the orange slice and cherry.

# French 75

SERVES 1

INGREDIENTS
1 fl oz (30 ml) gin
2 fl oz (60 ml) sweet-
and-sour mix (see
introduction)

Champagne

GLASS
9 fl oz (285 ml) highball
glass

1. Build over ice in glass and stir lightly. Top up with Champagne.

# Mai Tai

SERVES 1

INGREDIENTS
1 fl oz (30 ml) white rum
½ fl oz (15 ml) amaretto
½ fl oz (15 ml) dark rum
1 fl oz (30 ml) orange
curaçao
1 fl oz (30 ml) lemon juice
1 fl oz (30 ml) sugar syrup
(see introduction)

½ fl oz (15 ml) lime juice
wedge of pineapple
mint leaves

GLASS
9 fl oz (285 ml) hurricane
glass

1. Shake liquid ingredients with ice and pour into the glass. Garnish with pineapple wedge and mint leaves. Serve with a straw.

# Piña Colada

SERVES 1

*INGREDIENTS*
*1 fl oz (30 ml) light rum*
*1 fl oz (30 ml) coconut
cream*

*2 fl oz (60 ml) pineapple
syrup*

*1 pineapple spear*

*GLASS*
*9 fl oz (285 ml) highball
glass*

**1.** Blend first 3 ingredients with ice until mixed,
then pour into glass. Garnish with pineapple spear
and serve with a straw.

# Planter's Punch

SERVES 1

*INGREDIENTS*
*1 fl oz (30 ml) dark rum*
*½ fl oz (15 ml) grenadine*
*dash of Angostura bitters*
*1½ fl oz (45 ml) sweet-
and-sour mix (see
introduction)*

*soda water*
*1 cherry*

*GLASS*
*9 fl oz (285 ml) highball
glass*

**1.** Shake first 4 ingredients over ice and strain into
glass. Top up with soda water and stir. Garnish with
the cherry. Serve with a straw and stirrer.

# Singapore Sling

SERVES 1

INGREDIENTS
1 fl oz (30 ml) gin
2 fl oz (60 ml) sweet-
and-sour mix (see
introduction)

½ fl oz (15 ml) grenadine
½ fl oz (15 ml) cherry
brandy

1 cherry

GLASS
9 fl oz (285 ml) highball
glass

1. Build first 3 ingredients over ice in glass and stir
well. Top with cherry brandy and garnish with the
cherry. Serve with a stirrer.

# Tom Collins

SERVES 1

INGREDIENTS
2 fl oz (60 ml) lemon juice
1 tsp (5 ml) sugar
2 fl oz (60 ml) gin
soda water
slice of lemon
1 cherry

GLASS
9 fl oz (285 ml) highball
glass

1. Build the first 3 ingredients over ice in
the glass and stir. Top up with soda water, garnish
with the lemon slice and cherry. Serve with a straw
and stirrer.

# classics

# Bloody Mary

SERVES 1

INGREDIENTS
1 fl oz (30 ml) vodka
4 fl oz (120 ml) tomato juice
dash of Worcestershire sauce
few drops of Tabasco
salt and black pepper
1 stalk celery

1 stick cucumber
slice of lemon

GLASS
9 fl oz (285 ml) highball
glass

**1.** Shake liquid ingredients and salt and pepper over ice and pour into glass. Garnish with celery, cucumber and slice of lemon.

# Brandy Alexander

SERVES 1

INGREDIENTS
1 fl oz (30 ml) brandy
1 fl oz (30 ml) dark crème
    de cacao
1 fl oz (30 ml) double
    (heavy) cream

ground nutmeg
1 cherry

GLASS
5 fl oz (145 ml) cocktail
glass

**1.** Shake all ingredients except nutmeg and cherry with ice and strain into glass. Garnish with nutmeg, then skewer cherry with a cocktail stick and add to glass.

# Champagne Cocktail

SERVES 1

*INGREDIENTS*
*1 sugar cube*
*6 drops Angostura bitters*
*½ fl oz (15 ml) Cognac*
*4 fl oz (120 ml) Champagne*
*1 cherry*

*GLASS*
*5 fl oz (145 ml) Champagne flute*

**1.** Soak sugar cube in Angostura bitters in the flute before adding Cognac, then top with Champagne. Drop cherry into glass.

# Cosmopolitan

SERVES 1

*INGREDIENTS*
*1½ fl oz (45 ml) vodka*
*1 fl oz (30 ml) Cointreau*
*1 fl oz (30 ml) cranberry juice*
*½ fl oz (15 ml) freshly squeezed lime juice*

*wedge of lime*

*GLASS*
*5 fl oz (145 ml) cocktail glass*

**1.** Combine liquid ingredients in a cocktail shaker with cracked ice and shake well. Pour into a chilled glass. Garnish with the lime wedge.

# Daiquiri

*INGREDIENTS*
*1½ fl oz (45 ml) white rum*
*1 fl oz (30 ml) freshly
    squeezed lemon juice*
*½ fl oz (15 ml) sugar syrup
    (see introduction)*

*½ egg white (optional)*
*lemon twist*

*GLASS*
*5 fl oz (145 ml) Champagne
    saucer*

**1.**  Shake all ingredients except lemon spiral with ice and strain into Champagne saucer. Garnish with the lemon twist.

# Death in the Afternoon

SERVES 1

*INGREDIENTS*
*½ fl oz (15 ml) Pernod*
*4 fl oz (120 ml) Champagne*

*GLASS*
*5 fl oz (145 ml) Champagne
    flute*

**1.**  Pour Pernod into glass then fill with chilled Champagne.

# Fluffy Duck

SERVES 1

*INGREDIENTS*
*1 fl oz (30 ml) white rum*
*1 fl oz (30 ml) advocaat*
*lemonade*
*1¾ fl oz (40 ml) double*
*(heavy) cream*

*slice of orange*
*1 red cherry*

*GLASS*
*9 fl oz (285 ml) fancy*
*highball glass*

**1.** Build over ice and top up with lemonade to about a finger-width from top, then float the cream on top. Garnish with the orange slice and red cherry.

# Gibson

SERVES 1

*INGREDIENTS*
*2¼ fl oz (60 ml) gin*
*½ fl oz (15 ml) dry*
*vermouth*

*1 white cocktail onion*

*GLASS*
*3 fl oz (90 ml) cocktail glass*

**1.** Pour gin and vermouth into glass over ice and stir. Pierce onion with toothpick and drop into drink.

# Godfather

SERVES 1

INGREDIENTS

1 fl oz (30 ml) Scotch
  whisky

1 fl oz (30 ml) amaretto

GLASS

7 fl oz (200 ml) old-
  fashioned glass

1.  Pour into glass over ice and stir.


# Harvey Wallbanger

SERVES 1

INGREDIENTS

1 fl oz (30 ml) vodka
½ fl oz (15 ml) Galliano
4 fl oz (120 ml) orange juice
½ slice of orange
1 red cherry

GLASS

9 fl oz (285 ml) fancy
  highball glass

1.  Build over ice and top up with orange juice.
Garnish with the orange and red cherry.

# Long Island Iced Tea

SERVES 1

INGREDIENTS
1 fl oz (30 ml) vodka
1 fl oz (30 ml) tequila
1 fl oz (30 ml) white rum
½ fl oz (15 ml) Cointreau
1 fl oz (30 ml) lemon juice
1 fl oz (30 ml) sugar syrup
  (see introduction)

dash of cola
lemon twist
mint leaves

GLASS
9 fl oz (285 ml) fancy
  highball glass

**1.** Build over ice and top up with cola. Garnish with the lemon twist and mint leaves. Serve with a straw and stirrer.

# Manhattan

SERVES 1

INGREDIENTS
1½ fl oz (45 ml) Bourbon
1 fl oz (30 ml) sweet
  vermouth

dash of Angostura bitters

1 red cherry

GLASS
5 fl oz (145 ml) cocktail
  glass

**1.** Pour into glass over ice and stir, then strain into a clean glass. Garnish with the cherry on cocktail stick.

# Margarita

*INGREDIENTS*
*2 slices of lemon*
*salt*
*1 fl oz (30 ml) tequila*
*1 fl oz (30 ml) lemon juice*
*½ fl oz (15 ml) Cointreau*

*½ egg white (optional)*

*GLASS*
*5 fl oz (145 ml) margarita glass*

**1.** Rub rim of glass with 1 slice of lemon and frost with salt. Shake all ingredients except lemon with ice and strain into glass. Garnish with remaining lemon slice on side of glass.

# Martini

SERVES 1

*INGREDIENTS*
*1½ fl oz (45 ml) gin*
*1 fl oz (30 ml) dry vermouth*
*1 olive*

*GLASS*
*3 fl oz (90 ml) martini glass*

**1.** Pour into mixing glass over ice and stir, then strain into martini glass. Garnish with olive on toothpick.

# Mint Julep

SERVES 1

INGREDIENTS
1 tsp (5 ml) sugar
3 dashes of soda water
5 sprigs fresh mint
2 fl oz (60 ml) Bourbon

GLASS
9 fl oz (285 ml) fancy
highball glass

1.   Muddle sugar, soda water and 4 mint sprigs in a glass. Pour into chilled glass packed with ice. Add Bourbon and mix with a chopping motion using a long-handled bar spoon. Garnish with remaining mint and serve with a straw.

# Old-Fashioned Scotch

SERVES 1

INGREDIENTS
Angostura bitters
1 sugar cube
1 fl oz (30 ml) Scotch whisky
soda water
slice of lemon

slice of orange

GLASS
7 fl oz (200 ml) old-
fashioned glass

1.   Splash bitters evenly over sugar cube before adding ice and Scotch. Top up with soda water. Garnish with the slice of lemon and orange.

# Orgasm

SERVES 1

*INGREDIENTS*
1 fl oz (30 ml) Baileys
1 fl oz (30 ml) Cointreau
1 strawberry

*GLASS*
145 ml Champagne flute

**1.** Pour liquid ingredients into glass over ice and stir. Garnish with the strawberry on the side.

# Screwdriver

SERVES 1

*INGREDIENTS*
1½ fl oz (45 ml) vodka
1½ fl oz (45 ml) orange juice
slice of orange

*GLASS*
7 fl oz (200 ml) old-fashioned glass

**1.** Build over ice. Garnish with the orange.

# wines & punches

# Brazil Cocktail

SERVES 1

INGREDIENTS
1½ fl oz (45 ml) dry sherry
1½ fl oz (45 ml) dry
vermouth
dash of Angostura bitters
½ tsp (2.5 ml) ouzo

GLASS
5 fl oz (145 ml) tumbler

1. Place all ingredients in mixing glass with cracked ice, stir well and then strain into cocktail glass.

# Buck's Fizz

SERVES 1

INGREDIENTS
5 fl oz (145 ml) Champagne
½ fl oz (15 ml)Cointreau
1 fl oz (30 ml) orange juice
1½ tsp (7.5 ml grenadine
slice of orange

GLASS
7 fl oz (200 ml) Champagne
flute

1. Pour all ingredients except grenadine and orange slice into chilled Champagne flute. Drop the grenadine into centre of the drink and stir well. Garnish with the orange slice and serve with a straw.

# Claret Cobbler

SERVES 1

INGREDIENTS

2 fl oz (60 ml) soda water

1 tsp (5 ml) caster
   (superfine) sugar

3 fl oz (90 ml) claret

1 red grape

GLASS

7 fl oz (200 ml) red wine
   glass

**1.** Pour soda water over sugar in glass and stir until dissolved. Add claret, then fill glass with cracked ice and stir well. Serve with the grape on side of glass.

# Easter Bonnet

SERVES 1

INGREDIENTS

1½ fl oz (45 ml) apricot
   brandy

2 fl oz (60 ml) vodka

½ fl oz (15 ml fresh lime
   juice

dry Champagne

slice of lime

1 pineapple spear

GLASS

9 fl oz (230 ml) hurricane
   glass

**1.** Build over ice in hurricane glass, top up with Champagne and stir slowly. Garnish with lime and pineapple. Serve with a straw.

# Kir

INGREDIENTS
½ fl oz (15 ml) crème de
cassis

dry white wine

GLASS
5 fl oz (145 ml) white wine
glass

1. Pour crème de cassis into glass, then top up
with chilled dry white wine, no ice.

# Kir Royal

SERVES 1

INGREDIENTS
½ fl oz (15 ml) crème de
cassis

Champagne

GLASS
5 fl oz (145 ml) Champagne
flute

1. Pour crème de cassis into glass, then top up
with chilled Champagne, no ice.

NOTE
Kir Imperial is made with grenadine and crème de
cassis plus Champagne.

# Port Cocktail

SERVES 1

*INGREDIENTS*
*2½ fl oz (75 ml) port*
*1½ tsp (7.5 ml) brandy*

*GLASS*
*5 fl oz (145 ml) cocktail
glass*

1. Place ingredients in mixing glass with cracked ice, stir well, then strain into cocktail glass.

# Spritzer

SERVES 1

*INGREDIENTS*
*3 fl oz (90 ml) dry white
wine*

*soda water*

*GLASS*
*6 fl oz (180 ml) white wine
glass*

1. Pour chilled wine into glass, then top up with chilled soda water, no ice.

# Twelfth Night Champagne

SERVES 1

INGREDIENTS
slice of lime
caster (superfine) sugar
1 fl oz (30 ml) Grand
 Marnier
½ slice of lemon

½ slice of orange
dry Champagne

GLASS
5 fl oz (145 ml) Champagne
 flute

1.    Rub lime slice around rim of Champagne flute, then frost rim of glass with sugar. Pour Grand Marnier into glass, drop the 2 slices of fruit in and top up with chilled Champagne.

# Apple Punch

SERVES 1

INGREDIENTS
8 apples, cored and sliced
juice of 1 lemon
1¼ fl oz (40 ml) sugar
4 fl oz (120 ml) Calvados
2 bottles white wine

1 bottle soda water
1 bottle Champagne

SERVING BOWL
1 large punch bowl

1.    Place apples in punch bowl, drizzle lemon juice over and sprinkle with sugar. Refrigerate for 3–4 hours. Add Calvados and white wine and stir well. Add the soda water, Champagne and 4 cups ice cubes. Serve in cocktail glasses or Champagne flutes. Garnish with apple slices.

# Cold Duck

SERVES 10

*INGREDIENTS*
*2 bottles white wine*
*1 bottle sparkling wine*
*2 lemon peel spirals*

*SERVING BOWL*
*1 large punch bowl*

**1.** Pour all ingredients into punch bowl with 2 cups ice cubes and stir well. Serve in Champagne flutes or white wine glasses.

# Gin Punch

SERVES 10

*INGREDIENTS*
*1 bottle gin*
*5 cups (2 pints/1.2 litres)*
*  pineapple juice*

*5 cups (2 pints/1.2 litres)*
*  lemonade*

*2 fl oz (60 ml) lemon juice*

*4 cups 1¾ pints/1 litre)*
*  orange juice*

*selection of chopped fruit*

*SERVING BOWL*
*1 large punch bowl*

**1.** Pour all ingredients into punch bowl with 4 cups ice cubes and stir well. Serve in punch cups.

# Kiwi Punch

SERVES 10

INGREDIENTS
6 kiwi fruit, peeled and diced
2 nectarines, diced
1 fl oz (30 ml) dark rum
1 bottle dry white wine

4 cups (1¾ pints/1 litre)
  lemonade

SERVING BOWL
1 large punch bowl

**1.** Place the fruit into the punch bowl, pour the rum over the fruit, then cover and refrigerate for about 1 hour. Add wine and stir well. Add 4 cups ice cubes, then top up with the lemonade. Serve in wine glasses or punch mugs.

# Melon Punch

SERVES 10

INGREDIENTS
½ bottle melon liqueur
½ bottle vodka
4 cups (1¾ pints/1 litre)
  lemonade
2 cups (16 fl oz/475 ml )
  pineapple juice

selection of chopped fruit

SERVING BOWL
1 large punch bowl

**1.** Pour all ingredients into punch bowl with 2 cups ice cubes and stir well. Serve in white wine glasses.

# Old English Punch

SERVES 10

INGREDIENTS
2 bunches mint leaves
8 fl oz (250 ml) whisky
2 bottles white wine
2 bottles Champagne
selection of chopped fruit

SERVING BOWL
1 large punch bowl

1. Crumble mint leaves and place them in the bowl with 4 cups ice cubes, pour the whisky over and let stand for about 15 minutes. Pour all other ingredients into the punch bowl and stir well. Serve in cocktail glasses.

# Pineapple Punch

SERVES 10

INGREDIENTS
1 pineapple, peeled, cored and diced
1 lime, sliced
2 fl oz (60 ml) blue curaçao
2 fl oz (60 ml) dark rum

2 bottles dry white wine
1 bottle Champagne

SERVING BOWL
1 large punch bowl

1. Place the pineapple, lime, curaçao, rum and one bottle of white wine into the punch bowl, cover and refrigerate for about 3–4 hours. Add second bottle of wine and stir well. Add 4 cups ice cubes, then top up with the Champagne. Serve in cocktail glasses.

# Raspberry Lime Punch

SERVES 10

*INGREDIENTS*
*1 lb (450 g) raspberries*
*1 lime, sliced*
*40 g (1¾ oz) caster
    (superfine) sugar*

*2 bottles rosé wine*
*3 bottles Champagne*

*SERVING BOWL*
*1 large punch bowl*

**1.**   Place raspberries and lime slices into punch bowl. Sprinkle sugar over the fruit, cover and refrigerate for about half an hour. Add rosé and stir well. Add 4 cups ice cubes, then top up with the Champagne. Serve in cocktail glasses.

# Sangria

SERVES 10

*INGREDIENTS*
*1 bottle claret*
*2 fl oz (60 ml) brandy*
*2 fl oz (60 ml) white rum*
*2 fl oz (60 ml) Cointreau*
*4 cups (1¾ pints/1 litre)
    orange juice*

*2 tsp (10 ml) sugar*
*selection of chopped fruit*

*SERVING BOWL*
*1 large punch bowl*

**1.**   Pour all ingredients into punch bowl with 4 cups ice cubes and stir well. Serve in cocktail glasses.

# non-alcoholic

# Alice in Wonderland

SERVES 1

INGREDIENTS
3½ fl oz (100 ml) grapefruit
    juice

1 fl oz (30 ml) green tea
4 tsp (20 ml) lemon juice
½ fl oz (15 ml) sugar syrup
    (see introduction)

soda water
1 grape

GLASS
6 fl oz (180 ml) tulip
    cocktail glass

**1.** Build over ice and top up with soda water.
Garnish with a grape.

# Banapple Smoothie

SERVES 1

INGREDIENTS
4 fl oz (120 ml) milk
½ banana, sliced
½ apple, peeled
½ cup natural yoghurt
1 tsp (5 ml) honey

2–3 drops vanilla extract
sprinkles

GLASS
¾ pint (460 ml) fancy
    highball glass

**1.** Place all ingredients, except sprinkles and
1–2 slices of banana, in blender with 3 ice cubes and
blend until smooth. Pour into chilled glass, garnish
with sprinkles and reserved banana and serve.

# Banana Zing Smoothie

SERVES 1

INGREDIENTS
4 fl oz (120 ml) milk
½ banana
juice of 1 orange
3–4 drops lemon juice
4 fl oz (120 ml) natural
    yogurt

2 tsp (10 ml) apple juice
    concentrate
slice of orange

GLASS
460 ml hurricane glass

**1.** Place all ingredients except orange slice in blender with four ice cubes and blend until smooth. Pour into chilled glass and serve topped with a slice of orange and a straw.

# Banberry Smoothie

SERVES 1

INGREDIENTS
4 fl oz (120 ml) milk
½ banana
2 strawberries
½ apple, peeled
5–6 blueberries
4 fl oz (120 ml) natural
    yogurt

1 tsp (5 ml) honey
coloured sprinkles

GLASS
9 fl oz (285 ml) old-
    fashioned glass

**1.** Place all ingredients except orange slice in blender with four ice cubes and blend until smooth. Pour into chilled glass and serve topped with a slice of orange and a straw.

# Berry Banana Smoothie

SERVES 1

INGREDIENTS
6 frozen strawberries
10–12 blueberries
4 fl oz (120 ml) milk
1 banana
1 tsp (5 ml) honey

2 drops vanilla extract
vanilla sugar

GLASS
¾ pint (460 ml) fancy
 highball glass

1.   Reserve one strawberry and a few blueberries.
Place all remaining ingredients except sugar in blender
with four ice cubes and blend until smooth. Pour into chilled
glass and serve topped with reserved strawberry and blueberries, and a sprinkle of
vanilla sugar.

# Blunt Screwdriver

SERVES 1

INGREDIENTS
4 fl oz (120 ml) ginger ale
4 fl oz (120 ml) orange juice
slice of orange
1 red cherry

GLASS
9 fl oz (285 ml) highball
 glass

1.   Build over ice. Garnish with the orange slice and
red cherry.

NOTE
This cousin of the well-known alcoholic screwdriver
substitutes the ginger ale for vodka. Add ½ fl oz
(15 ml) grenadine for a Roy Rogers.

# Calypso Smoothie

SERVES 1

INGREDIENTS
pulp of 3 passionfruit
4 fl oz (120 ml) milk
2½ fl oz (75 ml) pineapple
    juice
½ banana

½ cup natural yoghurt
1 tsp (5 ml) honey

GLASS
460 ml hurricane glass

**1.** Reserve the pulp of 1 passionfruit. Place all remaining ingredients in blender with 4 ice cubes and blend until smooth. Pour into chilled glass and serve with a swirl of passionfruit pulp to garnish.

# Cranberry Zinger

SERVES 2

INGREDIENTS
4 fl oz (120 ml) cranberry
    juice
2 tsp (10 ml) brown sugar
1 tsp (5 ml) lemon extract
1 cup pineapple pieces

8 fl oz (250 ml) ginger ale

GLASS
9 fl oz (285 ml) footed
    highball glass

**1.** Combine all ingredients except ginger ale. Add ginger ale and ice before serving.

# Ginger Mick

INGREDIENTS
4 fl oz (120 ml) dry ginger
    ale

½ fl oz (15 ml) lime juice

1 fl oz (30 ml) Claytons
    Tonic

1 fl oz (30 ml) lemon juice

60 ml apple juice
slice of banana

GLASS
9 fl oz (285 ml) highball
    glass

**1.** Blend liquid ingredients with ice and pour into glass. Garnish with banana slices wedged on rim of glass.

# Mockatini

SERVES 1

INGREDIENTS
½ fl oz (15 ml) lime juice
dash of lemon juice
2 fl oz (60 ml) tonic water
1 green olive

GLASS
3 fl oz (90 ml) cocktail glass

**1.** Stir liquid ingredients with ice and strain. Garnish with a green olive on a toothpick or a lemon twist.

# Shirley Temple

SERVES 1

INGREDIENTS
½ fl oz (15 ml) grenadine
8 ½ fl oz (270 ml) ginger
    ale or
lemonade

slice of orange

GLASS
9 fl oz (285 ml) highball
    glass

**1.** Build over ice. Garnish with the slice of orange.

NOTE
For a tangy variation to this drink, try a Shirley Temple
No.2. Use 2 fl oz (60 ml) pineapple juice to a glass half-full of ice. Top with lemonade,
float ½ fl oz (15ml) passionfruit pulp on top and garnish with a pineapple wedge
and cherry.

# Strawberry Swirl

SERVES 1

INGREDIENTS
4 frozen strawberries
ground cinnamon
4 tablespoons strawberry
    topping

8 fl oz (250 ml) milk

GLASS
9 fl oz (285 ml) fancy
    highball glass

Place strawberries, cinnamon, 1 ice cube and half
the strawberry topping into a blender and blend
until an icy purée is formed. Place in a small bowl and
put in the freezer while you make the rest of the drink. Without rinsing the blender,
add the milk and remaining strawberry topping and blend until frothy. Spoon the
frozen pulp into the bottom of the glass and drizzle a little extra syrup around the
sides. Pour over the strawberry milkshake and serve.

# Index

First published 2013 by
New Holland Publishers Pty Ltd
London · Sydney · Cape Town · Auckland

Garfield House 86–88 Edgware Road London W2 2EA United Kingdom
1/66 Gibbes Street Chatswood NSW 2067 Australia
Wembley Square First Floor Solan Road Gardens Cape Town 8001 South Africa
218 Lake Road Northcote Auckland New Zealand

www.newhollandpublishers.com

A record of this book is held at the British Library and the National Library of Australia

ISBN 9781742573922

Publisher: Fiona Schultz
Designer: Lorena Susak
Production director: Olga Dementiev
Printer: Toppan Leefung Printing Limited

10 9 8 7 6 5 4 3 2 1

Keep up with New Holland Publishers on Facebook http://www.facebook.com/
NewHollandPublishers 

DISCLAIMER
Raw eggs are not suitable for consumption by pregnant women and the elderly.